John Prescott Biography

John Prescott Bi...

The Inspiring Journey of Britain's Longest-Serving Deputy Prime Minister

LINDSEY T. GORDON

John Prescott Biography

COPYRIGHT

All rights reserved. No part of this publication may be reproduced, distributed, or transmitted in any form or by any means, including photocopying, recording, or other electronic or mechanical methods, without the prior written permission of the publisher, except in the case of brief quotations embodied in critical reviews and certain other noncommercial uses permitted by copyright law.

Copyright © Lindsey T. Gordon, 2024.

John Prescott Biography

TABLE OF CONTENTS

INTRODUCTION..............................6
  The Legacy of John Prescott...................6
    Why His Story Matters....................... 8
    Overview of a Life Devoted to Public Service................................... 10

CHAPTER ONE..............................13
  Humble Beginnings............................. 13
    Growing Up in a Working-Class Family.. 15
    First Jobs: From Trainee Chef to Cunard Steward................................. 17

CHAPTER TWO.............................. 21
  From Sea to Politics............................. 21
    Joining the Trade Union Movement.. 24
    A New Path: Entering the Labour Party.. 26

CHAPTER THREE..........................30
  The Labour Climb...............................30
    The Kinnock Years: Rising in the Party.. 33

Balancing Modernisation and Tradition.. 36
CHAPTER FOUR............................41
The Deputy Prime Minister Years......... 41
Mediating Between Tony Blair and Gordon Brown.......................... 45
Championing Working-Class Values in a Modernising Party......... 50
CHAPTER FIVE.............................. 55
Key Political Achievements................... 55
Driving Transport Reforms.............. 59
Fighting for Social Justice................ 63
CHAPTER SIX................................69
Challenges and Controversies............... 69
Criticism of the Iraq War and New Labour Policies.................................74
Personal Struggles in the Public Eye..78
CHAPTER SEVEN.......................... 83
A Voice for the Working Class...............83
Defending Jeremy Corbyn's Leadership...87
Preserving Labour's Identity Amid Change.. 91

CHAPTER EIGHT..........................96
Life Beyond Politics.............................96
Reflections on the House of Lords and Retirement................................99
Health Struggles: The Stroke and Alzheimer's Battle.......................... 103

CHAPTER NINE.......................... 108
Tributes and Legacy............................108
International Recognition: Al Gore's Testimony............................ 113
The Lasting Impact on Labour and British Politics.........................117

CHAPTER TEN............................ 122
Lessons from a Life of Service............. 122
The Importance of Authenticity in Leadership....................................126
What Future Leaders Can Learn from John Prescott.........................130

CONCLUSION..............................136
Summing Up a Life Well-Lived........... 136
The Enduring Influence of John Prescott..138
Carrying Forward His Fight for Justice and Equality........................ 142

John Prescott Biography

INTRODUCTION

The Legacy of John Prescott

John Prescott's life is a testament to resilience, determination, and the power of authenticity in public service. As Britain's longest-serving Deputy Prime Minister, his career spanned over four decades, marked by tireless advocacy for the working class, groundbreaking environmental policies, and steadfast loyalty to his party. Born into a modest working-class family in Prestatyn, Wales, Prescott rose from humble beginnings to become a central figure in British politics.

Prescott's legacy is multifaceted: he is remembered as a bridge between New Labour's modernising agenda under Tony

Blair and the traditional values of the Labour movement. His contributions to environmental policies, such as his role in negotiating the Kyoto Protocol, showcased his global vision. Meanwhile, his blunt, no-nonsense demeanor and unapologetic defense of working-class interests made him a beloved figure among Labour's grassroots supporters.

Through moments of triumph and controversy, Prescott embodied the spirit of resilience. Whether mediating between Tony Blair and Gordon Brown during tense periods of Labour leadership or standing firm during public criticism, he never wavered in his commitment to the causes he held dear. His story is one of dedication, authenticity, and an unwavering belief in the transformative power of politics.

Why His Story Matters

The story of John Prescott is more than just a political biography; it is a window into the soul of modern British politics and a reminder of the enduring relevance of working-class voices in governance. In an era when political leaders are often accused of being out of touch with ordinary citizens, Prescott's life offers a powerful counter-narrative. His deep connection to his roots and ability to relate to the struggles of everyday people made him a unique figure in British political history.

Prescott's journey highlights the importance of inclusivity in politics. His presence alongside Tony Blair, a leader with an Oxbridge education and a polished demeanor, demonstrated the strength of diversity in leadership styles and backgrounds. Together, they formed a partnership that appealed to a broad spectrum of voters, helping Labour secure three consecutive electoral victories—a feat unmatched in modern British political history.

His story also matters because it reflects the challenges and rewards of navigating political life. Prescott was a man of contradictions: a staunch defender of social justice who faced criticism for his actions and decisions, and a man of humble beginnings who rose to the highest echelons of power without losing sight of his roots.

His ability to balance these contradictions offers valuable lessons for politicians and public servants today.

Overview of a Life Devoted to Public Service

John Prescott's life can be described as a relentless pursuit of justice, equality, and progress. From his early days as a trade union activist to his decades-long tenure as MP for Kingston upon Hull East, Prescott dedicated himself to improving the lives of others. His rise from a steward on the Cunard Line to the Deputy Prime Minister's office is a story of grit and perseverance, underpinned by a deep-seated belief in the potential of politics to create meaningful change.

John Prescott Biography

As a minister, Prescott's portfolio was vast and impactful. He played a key role in environmental policy, most notably in the negotiation of the Kyoto Protocol, which set the foundation for international climate action. Domestically, he championed transport reforms, regional development, and social housing initiatives, always with a focus on addressing inequalities and empowering marginalized communities.

Beyond his policy achievements, Prescott's personal story resonates as an example of resilience. His ability to overcome challenges—whether they were political rivalries, public controversies, or personal health battles—demonstrates an unwavering commitment to his principles and to the people he served.

John Prescott Biography

In the final years of his life, Prescott remained a vocal advocate for the causes he believed in, even as he faced health difficulties. His legacy, shaped by a lifetime of public service, serves as a reminder of the power of perseverance, authenticity, and dedication to one's principles in the face of adversity.

This introduction provides a foundation for exploring John Prescott's remarkable life, capturing the essence of his contributions and setting the stage for a deeper dive into the chapters of his inspiring journey.

John Prescott Biography

CHAPTER ONE

Humble Beginnings

John Prescott was born on May 31, 1938, in the coastal town of Prestatyn, Wales. Nestled in the scenic Vale of Clwyd, Prestatyn was far removed from the political epicenters of Britain, but it would become the backdrop for Prescott's formative years. His early environment was marked by the modesty and hard-working ethos of a community where most families, like his own, earned their living through blue-collar labor.

As the son of a railway signalman, Prescott grew up with a deep appreciation for discipline, structure, and perseverance. The steady rhythm of railway life mirrored the working-class values instilled in him from a young age: commitment, reliability, and service to others. These principles would shape his worldview and fuel his determination to rise above the limitations often imposed by his socioeconomic background.

Prestatyn itself, though small and unassuming, offered Prescott a glimpse of the resilience and camaraderie of close-knit communities. It was in these early days that he began to develop the strong sense of identity and loyalty that would later define his political career.

John Prescott Biography

Growing Up in a Working-Class Family

John Prescott's upbringing was deeply rooted in the working-class traditions of 20th-century Britain. His father, Bert Prescott, worked as a railway signalman, while his mother, Phyllis, managed the household. Life in the Prescott family was simple yet rich in values, with a strong emphasis on hard work and self-reliance.

The challenges of post-war Britain were acutely felt in households like Prescott's. Rationing and economic uncertainty shaped the daily lives of many families, including his. Despite these hardships, the Prescotts maintained a sense of optimism, relying on their community and each other for support. These early experiences of shared struggle and mutual aid deeply influenced Prescott's later political focus on social justice and the welfare of working families.

Education played a secondary role in Prescott's early life, as economic necessity often dictated that children contribute to their family's income at an early age. Leaving school at just 15 years old, he was keenly aware of the opportunities denied to many working-class children. This awareness would later fuel his desire to champion policies that created pathways for young people from disadvantaged backgrounds.

Prescott's upbringing also imbued him with a sense of solidarity and pride in his roots. He understood the dignity of labor and the aspirations of working-class families who sought better lives for their children. These values became the bedrock of his political philosophy and shaped his lifelong commitment to representing the voiceless and marginalized in society.

First Jobs: From Trainee Chef to Cunard Steward

After leaving school, John Prescott entered the workforce, eager to contribute to his family's income and find his place in the world. His first job was as a trainee chef, a role that introduced him to the demands of hospitality and service industries. Working long hours in a high-pressure environment, Prescott learned the importance of teamwork, discipline, and attention to detail—skills that would later serve him well in politics.

However, it was his time as a steward on the Cunard Line that truly broadened Prescott's horizons. Joining the iconic British shipping company, he became part of the crew aboard luxury ocean liners, including the Queen Mary and Queen Elizabeth. This experience not only provided him with a steady income but also exposed him to a world far removed from the industrial landscapes of Britain.

Working on these grand ships, Prescott interacted with people from diverse cultures and socioeconomic backgrounds. He witnessed firsthand the stark disparities between the lives of wealthy passengers and the working-class crew. These observations reinforced his sense of injustice and ignited a desire to challenge societal inequalities.

His time at sea also shaped his character in other ways. The long voyages demanded resilience and adaptability, qualities that would become hallmarks of his political career. Additionally, the camaraderie among the crew fostered a sense of solidarity that resonated with his own working-class roots.

While his career at Cunard might have seemed a world away from politics, it was during this period that Prescott's interest in labor rights began to take shape. Observing the conditions faced by his fellow crew members, he became involved in trade union activities, laying the groundwork for his future as a champion of workers' rights.

John Prescott's humble beginnings in Prestatyn, his upbringing in a hardworking family, and his early jobs as a chef and steward on the Cunard Line were the foundation of a life that would later be dedicated to public service. These formative experiences shaped his identity, values, and determination, setting him on a path to becoming one of the most influential figures in British politics.

CHAPTER TWO

From Sea to Politics

John Prescott's years as a merchant seaman were transformative, offering him a rare glimpse into a world far removed from the working-class life he had known in Prestatyn. Working on the Cunard Line, Prescott sailed on luxury liners such as the Queen Mary and Queen Elizabeth, which connected Britain to the rest of the world. These voyages exposed him to diverse cultures, international issues, and the stark inequalities between the elite passengers and the hardworking crew below deck.

As a steward, Prescott's duties were physically demanding, often requiring long hours of labor under strict conditions. The job demanded resilience and a strong work ethic—qualities that would later become hallmarks of his political career. Yet, it was also an experience that offered him education beyond the confines of the classroom. Through conversations with passengers and interactions with his colleagues, Prescott began to develop a global perspective, understanding the interconnectedness of economic systems and the universal struggles of the working class.

These voyages also provided Prescott with a deeper awareness of injustice. While the wealthy passengers enjoyed the opulence of first-class cabins, the conditions for the crew were far less glamorous. The rigid hierarchies aboard these ships mirrored the broader societal inequalities he had observed throughout his life. Witnessing this disparity fueled his growing commitment to advocating for the rights of workers and addressing social inequities.

The years at sea were also formative in shaping Prescott's character. The discipline required to maintain order on the ships, the camaraderie among the crew, and the ability to adapt to unpredictable circumstances prepared him for the often-unpredictable world of politics. In retrospect, Prescott often referred to this period as the foundation of his resilience and his understanding of leadership and teamwork.

Joining the Trade Union Movement

While working as a merchant seaman, Prescott became increasingly aware of the power dynamics between employers and employees. Witnessing the challenges faced by his colleagues—low wages, long hours, and limited job security—ignited a desire in him to fight for better conditions for workers. This desire led him to join the National Union of Seamen (NUS), marking the beginning of his lifelong commitment to the trade union movement.

Prescott's involvement in the NUS quickly grew beyond mere membership. His natural charisma and ability to articulate the concerns of his fellow workers earned him a reputation as a skilled negotiator and an effective advocate. He soon found himself taking on leadership roles within the union, where he was instrumental in organizing efforts to secure better pay and improved working conditions for seamen.

The trade union movement also introduced Prescott to the broader world of labor politics. He attended conferences, engaged with leaders of other unions, and began to see the interconnectedness of workers' struggles across industries. These experiences solidified his belief in collective action as a powerful tool for social change.

During this period, Prescott's political ideology began to take shape. Influenced by the union's emphasis on solidarity and social justice, he developed a belief in the need for systemic change to address the root causes of inequality. His work in the NUS was not just about securing immediate benefits for workers but also about creating a fairer society where everyone had the opportunity to thrive.

A New Path: Entering the Labour Party

John Prescott's transition from trade unionism to formal politics was a natural progression. His work with the National Union of Seamen had brought him into contact with prominent Labour Party figures, and he quickly realized that achieving broader societal change would require a political platform. Encouraged by colleagues and mentors, Prescott joined the Labour Party in the early 1960s, marking the beginning of a new chapter in his life.

John Prescott Biography

As a Labour Party member, Prescott initially focused on local issues, using his platform to advocate for the rights of workers in his community. His speeches and campaigns resonated with working-class voters, who saw in him a representative who truly understood their struggles. Prescott's authenticity, combined with his deep knowledge of labor issues, made him a rising star within the party.

In 1966, Prescott took the leap into parliamentary politics, successfully contesting the seat of Kingston upon Hull East. His victory was a significant milestone, not just for Prescott but also for the Labour Party, which gained a passionate advocate for working-class interests. As an MP, Prescott quickly established himself as a vocal and effective representative, earning respect from both his constituents and his colleagues in Parliament.

Prescott's entry into the Labour Party also marked the beginning of a broader political journey. Over the years, he would rise through the ranks, taking on increasingly influential roles and shaping the party's policies on issues ranging from transportation to environmental protection. Throughout it all, he remained deeply committed to the principles that had first drawn him to politics: social justice, equality, and the empowerment of ordinary people.

John Prescott's journey from the high seas to the halls of Parliament is a testament to his determination and unwavering commitment to making a difference. His experiences as a merchant seaman and trade unionist not only shaped his political beliefs but also provided him with the skills and perspectives needed to navigate the complexities of public life. In entering the Labour Party, Prescott found a platform to amplify his advocacy for workers' rights and to pursue his vision of a fairer, more equitable society.

CHAPTER THREE

The Labour Climb

John Prescott's political career took a pivotal turn in 1970 when he successfully contested the seat for Kingston upon Hull East, securing a position in the House of Commons. This was not just a personal victory, but also a significant moment in his life that marked his transition from trade union activism to formal parliamentary politics. Prescott's rise to political office was the result of years of hard work, dedication, and a deep commitment to representing the working-class communities he had always championed.

As a candidate, Prescott was deeply connected to the local working-class constituents of Kingston upon Hull East, and his message resonated with their aspirations for a better life. His authenticity and directness made him a compelling figure; he was not an establishment politician, but rather a man who had walked in the same shoes as his constituents. This relatability made him a trusted voice for the working-class people of Hull.

Prescott's successful bid for MP also underscored his evolving political philosophy. While his roots in the trade union movement remained integral to his identity, his entry into Parliament gave him a platform to expand his focus from purely labor rights to the broader issues of social and economic justice. He soon became known for his strong, no-nonsense approach in Parliament, delivering impassioned speeches on issues affecting ordinary citizens, such as workers' rights, housing, and regional economic inequality.

In his early years as an MP, Prescott developed a reputation as a tireless advocate for his constituents, never failing to raise their concerns in the House of Commons. He worked to secure funding for local projects and made a point to be present and available to the people who had elected him. This focus on his constituency would become a hallmark of Prescott's long tenure in Parliament.

John Prescott Biography

The Kinnock Years: Rising in the Party

John Prescott's rise within the Labour Party was closely tied to the leadership of Neil Kinnock, who became leader of the Labour Party in 1983. Prescott, a staunch advocate for the working-class left, found a natural ally in Kinnock. The early 1980s were a tumultuous period for Labour, as the party struggled with internal divisions, particularly between the moderates and the hard left. Prescott's pragmatic approach to politics helped him gain prominence in the party, especially as Kinnock began to steer the party towards a more centrist position.

As Kinnock's deputy, Prescott played a pivotal role in the party's efforts to modernize and rebrand itself. Kinnock's leadership focused on rebuilding Labour's credibility, which had been severely damaged by the party's perceived extremism and internal chaos. Prescott, with his background in trade unions and his unapologetic working-class roots, provided the party with a crucial link to its traditional supporters, especially in the industrial heartlands.

His presence gave the Labour leadership an authentic voice that resonated with ordinary people, providing an important counterbalance to the more technocratic, middle-class wing of the party.

During this period, Prescott began to develop a reputation as a bold and outspoken figure within the party. He became known for his fiery speeches, combative style, and loyalty to Kinnock, even as the party faced electoral defeats. Despite the setbacks, Prescott's role in the party's attempts at modernization set the stage for his future influence within the Labour movement.

Kinnock's leadership saw Labour begin to regain ground, especially with the party's shift towards a more moderate and pragmatic stance. Prescott's close relationship with Kinnock allowed him to play a significant part in shaping the party's direction, even as the broader Labour Party debated how best to navigate the changing political landscape of Britain.

Balancing Modernisation and Tradition

One of the central tensions within the Labour Party during Prescott's rise was the balance between modernizing the party to appeal to a broader electorate and remaining true to its traditional working-class values. Prescott found himself at the center of this debate, particularly as Tony Blair's leadership in the 1990s sought to push the party further towards the center.

While Prescott was a firm supporter of Labour's traditional values, such as social justice and workers' rights, he recognized the need for the party to modernize in order to remain competitive in a rapidly changing political environment.

John Prescott Biography

In the early days of Tony Blair's leadership, Prescott was tasked with navigating the difficult waters between the party's left-wing base and its move towards the center. As the Deputy Leader of the Labour Party under Blair, Prescott was seen as a crucial figure who could maintain the connection to Labour's traditional working-class roots while supporting the leadership's vision of a more modern, electable party. His role in this period was to serve as the bridge between the party's new, more moderate policies and its historical base of support.

Prescott was particularly instrumental in shaping Labour's stance on issues related to economic inequality, education, and healthcare. While he supported the modernizing policies of Blair, such as the introduction of market-driven reforms, Prescott consistently fought to ensure that the party's traditional values of social equality and public welfare remained at the core of its agenda. His ability to maintain this delicate balance between modernisation and tradition made him one of the most important figures within the Labour Party during the 1990s and early 2000s.

The internal debates over this balance were not without their tensions. Prescott, as a man of deep principle, did not always agree with every policy shift under Blair's leadership, particularly as the party moved further away from its left-wing roots. However, Prescott's loyalty to the Labour Party and his commitment to its core values ensured that he remained a prominent and respected figure throughout these years.

By the time the 1997 general election arrived, Prescott had helped lead the Labour Party to an overwhelming victory. The party's success was, in part, due to the careful balancing act Prescott had performed between Labour's traditional base and the modern, centrist policies championed by Blair. It was clear that while Prescott was a staunch advocate for the working-class and its rights, he understood the importance of adapting to the changing political landscape in order to achieve tangible results.

John Prescott's climb within the Labour Party was marked by his unwavering commitment to working-class values, his skillful navigation of the tensions between modernization and tradition, and his ability to rise through the ranks under the leadership of Neil Kinnock and Tony Blair.

His work during these formative years laid the groundwork for his future as one of the most influential figures in British politics. His ability to balance loyalty to his roots with a pragmatic vision for the future made him an essential force within the Labour movement.

CHAPTER FOUR

The Deputy Prime Minister Years

The partnership between Tony Blair and John Prescott was often described as an unlikely one. In many ways, they seemed to be polar opposites: Blair, the polished, middle-class former barrister, and Prescott, the working-class former merchant seaman and trade unionist.

Despite these differences, the two formed a political duo that would go on to reshape British politics during the New Labour era. Their relationship was one of mutual respect, but also of tensions, with Prescott frequently playing the role of the gruff, straight-talking counterpoint to Blair's more controlled and diplomatic style.

Blair and Prescott's collaboration was key to New Labour's success in the 1990s, particularly during the 1997 general election, where the party won a landslide victory. Blair's vision of a modernized Labour Party—centered on economic prosperity, social justice, and international coopcration—was complemented by Prescott's commitment to social equality, workers' rights, and a strong connection to traditional Labour values.

Prescott's presence provided the necessary link to Labour's roots, ensuring that the party didn't lose touch with its working-class supporters as it sought to become more electorally appealing.

John Prescott Biography

In many ways, the pairing of Blair and Prescott became emblematic of the New Labour project. Blair was the face of modernization, pushing forward economic reforms and a centrist agenda, while Prescott was the voice of Labour's core values, ensuring that the party remained grounded in its principles of fairness, equality, and social justice. Together, they represented a balancing act between tradition and modernity, helping Labour craft policies that appealed to both the party's traditional base and a broader electorate.

Despite the apparent harmony in their public partnership, the relationship between Blair and Prescott was not without its tensions. Prescott, with his blunt manner and working-class sensibilities, was occasionally frustrated by Blair's smooth political maneuvering and his commitment to market-driven policies.

However, these differences were often mitigated by Prescott's loyalty to the Labour Party and his understanding of the bigger picture. While Prescott occasionally criticized elements of Blair's policy agenda, particularly regarding economic and foreign policy, he remained a staunch ally of Blair's leadership, recognizing that their combined efforts had achieved historic political victories.

Their partnership was also marked by a shared commitment to public service. Both Blair and Prescott were driven by the desire to improve the lives of ordinary people, albeit in different ways. Blair's policy goals often focused on economic growth, social inclusion, and international cooperation, while Prescott's efforts centered on improving the lives of working-class Britons and ensuring that Labour's historic values were not lost in the rush to modernize. Together, they provided the Labour Party with a dynamic leadership that was both progressive and grounded in its traditional roots.

Mediating Between Tony Blair and Gordon Brown

One of John Prescott's most critical roles during his time as Deputy Prime Minister was serving as a mediator between Tony Blair and Gordon Brown, the Chancellor of the Exchequer. The relationship between Blair and Brown was famously fractious, marked by years of rivalry and tension. While they were both aligned in their desire to modernize the Labour Party, their differing visions for the country often led to public disagreements and private struggles. Prescott, with his political savvy and longstanding experience in dealing with disputes, often found himself in the position of mediator between the two men.

As a key figure in New Labour, Prescott had the unique ability to relate to both Blair and Brown, and he understood the deeper dynamics that underpinned their relationship. Blair, the charismatic leader, was often more willing to embrace change and compromise, while Brown, with his more ideological approach, was deeply committed to ensuring that Labour's economic policies were rooted in the values of social democracy. This tension frequently spilled over into public view, with Blair's more centrist policies sometimes clashing with Brown's more traditional Labour stance.

Prescott's role as mediator was vital in maintaining the unity of the government, especially during the early years of Blair's premiership. He often worked behind the scenes to ensure that both men could maintain their influence within the party and the government, while keeping their disagreements from becoming public spectacles. Prescott's ability to act as a go-between helped to ease tensions and ensure that the party's agenda continued to move forward.

At times, Prescott's interventions helped to defuse potentially explosive situations. He would provide Blair and Brown with a sounding board, helping them to see each other's perspectives and find common ground. His practical approach to problem-solving, grounded in his working-class background, made him an effective intermediary.

He understood that both men's priorities—Blair's desire for political success and Brown's commitment to economic reform—were essential to the Labour Party's overall success. By keeping both men in check and helping them to navigate their differences, Prescott helped to prevent infighting that could have undermined Labour's achievements.

However, the strain between Blair and Brown was never fully resolved, and Prescott often found himself caught between the two powerful figures. While Prescott was loyal to Blair, he also understood the importance of Brown's role in shaping Labour's economic policies. His efforts as mediator were not always successful in preventing tensions from escalating, but his ability to navigate the complex political landscape helped to ensure that Labour's agenda remained on track.

Championing Working-Class Values in a Modernising Party

Throughout his tenure as Deputy Prime Minister, John Prescott remained a staunch champion of working-class values, even as New Labour sought to modernize and appeal to a broader electorate. Prescott's role in the government was to ensure that Labour's traditional principles of fairness, social justice, and equality were not lost amid the party's move toward the center. This often put him in a difficult position, as he had to reconcile the demands of modernity with the party's historical roots.

Prescott's work was grounded in the belief that a modernized Labour Party should not abandon its commitment to the working class. While Blair's leadership emphasized economic growth, internationalism, and public service reform, Prescott fought to ensure that the government did not neglect the needs of ordinary workers, particularly those in industrial communities.

He used his position to advocate for policies that would benefit working-class Britons, such as improving public transport, securing better housing, and advocating for social welfare programs that addressed poverty and inequality.

Prescott also played a key role in the development of the Labour Party's policies on the environment. As Secretary of State for the Environment, Transport, and the Regions, he championed efforts to address climate change and promote sustainable development, securing the UK's commitment to the Kyoto Protocol.

This was a particularly important moment in Prescott's career, as he was able to align his environmental advocacy with his long-standing belief in social justice. Prescott saw climate change not only as an environmental issue but also as an issue of economic justice, recognizing that the impacts of global warming disproportionately affected the world's poorest populations.

Despite his support for New Labour's modernization agenda, Prescott never lost sight of his roots. He frequently spoke out against policies that he believed would hurt the working class or undermine the party's commitment to fairness and equality.

His direct, often combative style ensured that the voices of the working-class people he represented were heard, even as the party moved toward the center. Prescott was a reminder to his colleagues that modernization should not come at the expense of Labour's core values, and that the party's success depended on staying true to the people it was created to represent.

John Prescott's time as Deputy Prime Minister was marked by his fierce dedication to working-class values, his role as a mediator between Tony Blair and Gordon Brown, and his ability to navigate the tensions of a rapidly modernizing

Labour Party. His contributions to New Labour were essential in maintaining the party's commitment to social justice and fairness, while also helping it adapt to the changing political landscape.

Prescott's leadership ensured that Labour's traditional values remained central to its agenda, even as it sought to become a more inclusive and electorally successful party.

CHAPTER FIVE

Key Political Achievements

One of John Prescott's most significant achievements during his tenure as Deputy Prime Minister was his role in championing environmental policies, particularly his pivotal involvement in securing the United Kingdom's commitment to the Kyoto Protocol in 1997.

As the Secretary of State for the Environment, Transport, and the Regions, Prescott was at the forefront of international efforts to combat climate change. The Kyoto Protocol, an international treaty aimed at reducing global greenhouse gas emissions, was a monumental step in global environmental governance, and Prescott played a key role in negotiating and ensuring that the UK ratified it.

Prescott's involvement in the Kyoto talks was a defining moment in his career, and it showcased his ability to work on the international stage while staying true to his core values. He understood that climate change was not only an environmental issue but also a matter of economic justice, particularly for the working-class communities he had long represented.

Prescott saw climate change as a problem that could disproportionately affect the poorest people, both in the UK and abroad, and he was determined to make sure that environmental policies did not just serve the affluent but also contributed to a fairer, more equitable society.

His work on the Kyoto Protocol came at a time when the global community was beginning to recognize the urgency of climate action. Prescott's leadership helped to establish the UK as a key player in international environmental negotiations, positioning Britain as a leader in the fight against climate change.

The success of the Kyoto talks, in which the UK played a critical role, was an achievement that Prescott could look back on with immense pride. It was not only a diplomatic victory but also an example of how Prescott's passion for social justice and his commitment to working-class communities informed his environmental advocacy.

Prescott believed that addressing climate change and securing environmental sustainability should be part of a broader agenda to combat inequality and improve the quality of life for all people, especially the most vulnerable.

Prescott's advocacy for environmental issues extended beyond international treaties. He also pushed for domestic policies that sought to make transport systems more sustainable and reduce the UK's carbon footprint. His work on the Kyoto Protocol laid the groundwork for future environmental initiatives under New Labour and established Prescott as one of the most influential voices in the UK's environmental movement during the late 1990s and early 2000s.

Driving Transport Reforms

John Prescott's influence on transport policy during his time as Deputy Prime Minister and Secretary of State for the Environment, Transport, and the Regions was substantial. A passionate advocate for improving public transport, Prescott recognized that an efficient, accessible, and sustainable transport system was critical to improving the lives of working-class people. He was instrumental in pushing forward several key transport reforms, which would have lasting impacts on the country's infrastructure and public services.

One of Prescott's key transport initiatives was the development of the Integrated Transport White Paper, published in 1998. The White Paper laid the foundations for a more sustainable transport policy that sought to reduce congestion, improve public transportation, and make transport systems more eco-friendly. Prescott's push for integrated transport aimed to connect cities and regions more efficiently while reducing the environmental impact of travel.

This vision would later result in the expansion of bus services, the development of light rail systems, and a push for greener alternatives to private car use. Prescott's focus on public transport was driven by a commitment to reducing social exclusion and making it easier for people, especially those from disadvantaged communities, to access work, education, and social services.

Prescott's time as Secretary of State also saw the controversial decision to introduce a national road pricing scheme. This plan, which sought to reduce traffic congestion by charging motorists based on the distance they traveled, was part of a broader effort to create a more sustainable and equitable transport system. While the proposal faced significant opposition from various political groups and the public, Prescott remained committed to the principle that a comprehensive, well-designed transport system could improve both environmental outcomes and the quality of life for ordinary Britons.

Additionally, Prescott worked on improving the rail industry, with significant investment directed toward modernizing the country's aging rail infrastructure. Under his leadership, the government pursued the development of high-speed rail lines, with the aim of increasing connectivity between major cities and offering an alternative to car and air travel.

While the challenges of rail privatization loomed over much of the sector, Prescott's determination to improve services and reduce the environmental impact of transportation led to policies that laid the groundwork for the modern rail network that would continue to evolve in the following decades.

Prescott's legacy in transport reform is one of forward-thinking policies aimed at creating a more sustainable and equitable system. He understood that for Labour to remain relevant to working-class voters, it had to deliver practical solutions to real-world problems, such as long commutes, expensive car ownership, and limited public transport options. His reforms continue to shape the UK's approach to transportation today.

Fighting for Social Justice

A cornerstone of John Prescott's political career was his relentless commitment to social justice. Throughout his decades in public life, Prescott remained an advocate for policies that sought to reduce inequality, improve working-class living conditions, and ensure equal opportunities for all. His social justice agenda was shaped by his own experiences growing up in a working-class family in Wales, and it informed many of the decisions he made as a senior figure in the Labour government.

As Deputy Prime Minister, Prescott was deeply committed to addressing the needs of the working class. He believed that government should be a force for equality, advocating for policies that would improve the lives of those who had been historically marginalized or overlooked. One of Prescott's primary goals was to ensure that economic prosperity was shared by all sections of society, not just the wealthy elite. His work on public services, such as education, housing, and health care, reflected this commitment to reducing inequality.

Prescott was also a passionate defender of workers' rights and the trade union movement. Having been involved in trade unions for much of his life, Prescott understood the importance of organized labor in achieving social justice. He worked hard to ensure that Labour's policies would support the rights of workers, particularly in the face of economic globalization and the rise of low-wage work.

He also fought for fair wages, better working conditions, and the protection of public services from privatization. As a result, he became a key figure in defending Labour's traditional values while pushing for necessary modernization.

One of Prescott's most notable achievements in social justice was his advocacy for urban regeneration. Recognizing that many working-class communities were suffering from underinvestment and social deprivation, he championed projects aimed at revitalizing neglected areas.

Through his work as Secretary of State for the Environment, Transport, and the Regions, Prescott helped to direct government resources to regenerate deprived areas, creating jobs and improving local infrastructure. His efforts in this area were designed to give communities the tools they needed to improve their own lives, rather than relying solely on top-down solutions.

Prescott's social justice work also extended internationally. As a supporter of fair trade and development aid, Prescott used his position to raise awareness about global poverty and the economic systems that perpetuated it. He was outspoken in his belief that the developed world had a responsibility to help lift up the global poor, and his work in international forums reflected this commitment.

John Prescott's key political achievements—his involvement in securing the Kyoto Protocol, driving transport reforms, and fighting for social justice—demonstrate the breadth of his legacy. From climate change to workers' rights, Prescott's policies sought to create a more sustainable, fair, and equitable society.

His ability to work across different sectors and his unwavering commitment to social justice made him one of the most significant political figures of his generation. Through his achievements, Prescott left an indelible mark on British politics and the Labour Party, ensuring that the values of equality and fairness continued to guide the party's direction for years to come.

CHAPTER SIX

Challenges and Controversies

One of the most memorable and controversial moments in John Prescott's career occurred during the 2001 general election campaign, when he famously punched a protester who threw an egg at him. The incident, which took place in Rhyl, North Wales, captured the media's attention and became a symbol of Prescott's fiery temperament and no-nonsense approach to politics.

It also sparked a wider debate about the role of political leaders in maintaining composure under pressure, and whether Prescott's reaction was a moment of lost control or a genuine display of working-class authenticity.

Prescott had always been known for his directness, and throughout his political career, he was unafraid to express his views in blunt terms. However, the egg-throwing incident was different—it was a rare moment of physical confrontation. The protester, who had thrown the egg at Prescott, was immediately confronted by the Deputy Prime Minister, who, in a moment of frustration and anger, punched him in the chest.

While the event became an infamous headline, it also exposed Prescott's deep sense of loyalty and protectiveness, both toward his political beliefs and his party.

Prescott, who had always been a staunch defender of the Labour movement and working-class values, saw the protester's actions as an insult not just to him personally, but to the values he represented. For many, the egg incident highlighted Prescott's authenticity in an increasingly sanitized and scripted political environment.

While some viewed it as an unprofessional and inappropriate reaction, others saw it as a genuine, visceral response to the sort of disrespect that many working-class individuals were familiar with in their everyday lives. Prescott's critics argued that the act was unbecoming of a senior politician and reflected a lack of self-control, while his supporters defended the punch as a sign of his down-to-earth, working-class roots, which made him relatable to ordinary voters.

In the years following the incident, Prescott's candid admission that he had acted impulsively and out of frustration did little to quell the public debate. He admitted that it was a "moment of madness," but also remarked that he was not going to apologize for defending himself and his political integrity.

The egg incident became a defining moment in Prescott's legacy, illustrating both his vulnerability and his commitment to fighting for the working-class people he represented. In a political culture that often prizes calculated responses and political spin, Prescott's raw and human reaction stood in stark contrast to the more polished image of many of his contemporaries.

Ultimately, the egg incident was not only a controversy but also a glimpse into Prescott's personal character—a politician who, despite his high office, never lost touch with the grit and determination that characterized his working-class background. It may have been an unscripted and chaotic moment, but it encapsulated Prescott's authenticity and his willingness to engage with both the public and the media on his own terms.

Criticism of the Iraq War and New Labour Policies

As a key member of Tony Blair's government, John Prescott was an enthusiastic supporter of the New Labour agenda, which sought to modernize the Labour Party and align it with more centrist policies.

However, the Iraq War, which began in 2003, would be a defining issue that would not only challenge Prescott's loyalty to Blair but also lead to significant criticism of the New Labour project as a whole. Prescott was one of the few senior Labour figures who publicly expressed discomfort with the war, and his position on the matter became a source of tension within both the party and his own personal conscience.

When the Blair government decided to join the United States in the invasion of Iraq, Prescott initially supported the decision, citing the need to disarm Saddam Hussein and the potential threat he posed to global security. However, as the war dragged on and the consequences became more apparent, Prescott's support for the conflict began to waver.

Many Labour Party members and critics within the public saw the war as a misguided decision based on questionable intelligence and the questionable motives of the Bush administration. Prescott, who had spent much of his career advocating for peace and justice, found himself in an increasingly difficult position as the situation in Iraq deteriorated.

By 2004, Prescott became one of the few Labour figures to openly voice opposition to the war. He publicly criticized the invasion, arguing that the aftermath of the conflict had been mishandled, and he expressed regret over his initial support. Prescott's criticism of the Iraq War was controversial, as it challenged the New Labour leadership's stance on foreign policy and their unwavering support for the American-led intervention.

Prescott's opposition to the war did not entirely break with Blair, but it marked a significant divergence in their political views, and it alienated some members of the Labour Party who felt that Prescott had failed to stand up to Blair's decisions from the outset.

This shift in Prescott's stance came at a time when public opposition to the war was growing, and the Labour government was facing increased criticism both from within and outside the party. Prescott's decision to criticize the war aligned him more closely with grassroots activists and anti-war movements, many of whom had been vocal in their opposition to the Iraq invasion from the beginning. It also reinforced the idea that Prescott, despite his loyalty to Blair and New Labour, was not afraid to challenge the party leadership when he believed a policy was wrong.

The Iraq War controversy left a lasting impact on Prescott's political career. His public criticism of the war, coupled with the growing dissatisfaction with New Labour's domestic and foreign policies, contributed to a shift in public perception of both Prescott and the Labour government.

The war became a turning point that ultimately led to a reassessment of New Labour's legacy, with many questioning whether the policies that had once made the government so popular were now failing to deliver the progressive change that many had hoped for.

Personal Struggles in the Public Eye

Throughout his long political career, John Prescott faced numerous personal struggles that were often laid bare for public consumption. His personal challenges, which included the breakdown of his marriage to his wife Pauline and the public scrutiny of his private life, played out in the media and were a source of both sympathy and derision. Prescott, like many public figures, was subject to intense scrutiny, and his personal life often intersected with his political career, resulting in a complex narrative of vulnerability and resilience.

One of the most publicized personal struggles Prescott faced was his extramarital affair with his secretary, which became the subject of tabloid headlines in 2006. The revelation of the affair was deeply damaging to Prescott's personal life and public image, and it created tensions within his marriage. The media's focus on his personal failings contrasted with the broader political challenges Prescott was facing at the time. Although Prescott publicly acknowledged the affair and expressed regret, the scandal became emblematic of the intense personal pressure that public figures, particularly in high office, often face.

At the same time, Prescott's relationship with his wife Pauline, who had been a steadfast supporter throughout his career, was also subject to public scrutiny. The couple's enduring partnership, despite the scandal, became a focal point for discussions about loyalty, forgiveness, and the human side of political figures. Pauline's own resilience and support for Prescott were often overshadowed by the media frenzy, but she remained a constant figure in his life, providing a sense of stability amid the turmoil.

Additionally, Prescott's health struggles, including his stroke in 2019 and his subsequent battle with Alzheimer's, were another source of personal difficulty. As a public figure who had spent decades in the limelight, Prescott's health decline was particularly poignant, and it raised important questions about the physical and emotional toll of public service.

Despite these challenges, Prescott maintained a sense of dignity and purpose, continuing to engage in political discourse and remaining a vocal advocate for the causes he believed in, even in the face of his own health struggles.

John Prescott's career was shaped by both his political successes and the personal and professional challenges he faced. The controversies surrounding the egg incident, his criticism of the Iraq War, and his personal struggles in the public eye illustrated the complexity of his character.

Prescott's ability to navigate these challenges while remaining true to his working-class roots and his commitment to social justice marked him as one of the most distinctive and human figures in British politics. Despite the controversies that surrounded him, Prescott's legacy remains one of authenticity, resilience, and a determination to fight for the values he believed in.

CHAPTER SEVEN

A Voice for the Working Class

Throughout his political career, John Prescott remained a staunch advocate for the working class, a constituency he never lost sight of, even as he rose to the highest echelons of British politics. Prescott's appeal lay in his authenticity and his ability to connect with ordinary people.

A product of the working-class communities of Hull and a representative of those values in Westminster, Prescott embodied the voice of the common man within a party that was, at times, seen as increasingly disconnected from its grassroots.

Prescott's political philosophy was firmly rooted in his belief in social justice and his commitment to improving the lives of working people. From the start of his political career, he made it clear that his allegiance was to those who worked hard to make a living but often faced adversity and marginalization. This connection with Labour's traditional base helped secure Prescott's place as one of the most important and influential figures in the Labour movement.

His tenure as Deputy Prime Minister during the New Labour years was marked by his focus on issues that resonated with working-class voters, including improving public services, creating more affordable housing, and fighting for fair wages.

Prescott's down-to-earth manner and blunt approach helped him build a strong rapport with ordinary people who saw in him someone who understood their struggles and frustrations.

Prescott's working-class roots provided a contrast to many of his fellow Labour politicians, who came from more privileged backgrounds. His straightforward style and sometimes fiery rhetoric stood in stark contrast to the more technocratic and media-savvy image that Tony Blair cultivated. While Blair was seen as a modernizer, with a vision of Labour that looked forward to a globalized, market-driven world, Prescott was a reminder of the party's roots in trade unionism, social welfare, and economic fairness. He was able to bridge the gap between Labour's traditional working-class support and the party's more progressive policies.

As the party underwent significant transformations under New Labour, Prescott remained a symbol of the old Labour ethos. His role as Deputy Prime Minister allowed him to influence key policies, but it was his unwavering connection to Labour's traditional base that made him an invaluable figure. For many, Prescott was a living reminder that Labour was still a party of the people, even as it navigated the challenges of modernization and the pressures of neoliberal economic policies.

Defending Jeremy Corbyn's Leadership

As the Labour Party evolved, especially during the leadership of Jeremy Corbyn from 2015 to 2020, Prescott found himself in a position where his loyalty to the party's working-class roots led him to support a more left-wing vision of Labour.

Corbyn's leadership was deeply divisive within the party, with many in the Blairite wing of Labour seeing him as a throwback to more radical days and a danger to the party's future. However, Prescott, ever loyal to the working-class values that had defined his career, publicly defended Corbyn and his leadership despite the tensions within the party.

Prescott was a vocal supporter of Corbyn's left-wing agenda, which included nationalizing key industries, reinvesting in public services, and implementing a more progressive tax system. He saw Corbyn as a figure who had managed to reconnect Labour with the working-class voters it had lost in the years since New Labour's modernization under Blair. For Prescott, Corbyn's election represented a return to the party's true values and an opportunity to fight for the people who had been left behind by successive governments, including Labour ones.

One of Prescott's key arguments in favor of Corbyn was that his leadership offered a genuine alternative to the establishment politics of both the Conservative Party and the centrist wing of Labour.

Prescott's experience as a working-class politician made him appreciate Corbyn's authenticity, his commitment to social justice, and his rejection of the neoliberal economic consensus that had dominated both British and global politics for decades. Prescott argued that Corbyn's leadership was an important step toward reasserting the Labour Party as the champion of ordinary people, rather than an institution that merely catered to the political and economic elite.

Despite Corbyn's controversial policies and the criticisms leveled at him from various factions of the Labour Party, Prescott's support for him was unyielding. He viewed Corbyn as the antithesis of the "business-as-usual" politics that had come to dominate the political landscape. Corbyn's focus on policies like climate action, social equality, and a more robust welfare state aligned with the values Prescott had fought for throughout his own political career.

Prescott's defense of Corbyn was not without personal cost. It put him at odds with many of his former colleagues, particularly those who had been aligned with Blair and New Labour. Yet, for Prescott, it was a reflection of his lifelong commitment to Labour's roots, to social justice, and to standing up for those whose voices had long been ignored in the corridors of power.

Preserving Labour's Identity Amid Change

Throughout the ups and downs of his political career, John Prescott was acutely aware of the changing dynamics within the Labour Party. From its inception as a party of working-class people to its evolution into New Labour under Tony Blair, Prescott saw the party undergo significant transformations. However, no matter how much the party changed, he always remained a vocal advocate for preserving the values that had defined Labour from its founding: fairness, equality, and a commitment to social justice.

John Prescott Biography

During the years when New Labour's centrist policies were dominant, Prescott was a crucial figure in ensuring that Labour retained a sense of connection with its traditional support base. He fought to preserve Labour's identity as the party of the working class, even as Blair modernized the party to appeal to middle-class voters and corporate interests.

Prescott believed that, despite the necessary changes and reforms within the party, the heart of Labour's identity had to remain focused on improving the lives of ordinary people and fighting for a fairer society.

As the Labour Party shifted again under Corbyn's leadership, Prescott saw an opportunity to return to the party's roots, which had been diluted during the New Labour years. For him, the question was never whether Labour needed to change—it was about ensuring that the party's fundamental principles were not lost in the process. He believed that Labour should be a party that reflected the diverse needs of the British public, but also one that stayed true to its working-class heritage. His defense of the party's core identity was a key part of his political legacy.

Prescott's efforts to preserve Labour's identity amid change also extended to his views on the relationship between Labour and the trade unions. The union movement, which had always been a vital part of Labour's foundation, was an issue close to Prescott's heart. He saw trade unions as the backbone of the Labour Party, both in terms of membership and values.

Throughout his career, Prescott worked to maintain the connection between the party and the unions, believing that Labour's strength lay in its ability to represent the working people who were often excluded from the mainstream political conversation.

Prescott's insistence on keeping Labour's identity intact, despite the pressures to modernize and appeal to new voter bases, ultimately positioned him as a guardian of the party's soul. He understood that change was necessary in politics, but he also understood the risks of losing sight of the very people the party was created to represent. His work to preserve Labour's identity through turbulent times, especially during the leaderships of Blair and Corbyn, made him a crucial figure in the ongoing history of the party.

In the end, John Prescott's legacy is defined by his unwavering commitment to the working class and his dedication to preserving the Labour Party's core mission: creating a fairer, more just society for all. Whether through his support of Corbyn's leadership or his ability to navigate Labour's evolution, Prescott remained a key figure in the party's story, a voice for the people who had long believed in Labour's promise of social equality.

John Prescott Biography

CHAPTER EIGHT

Life Beyond Politics

Even after stepping down from front-line politics, John Prescott remained an influential figure in public life, using his platform to advocate for causes close to his heart. Chief among these was his commitment to tackling climate change.

As Deputy Prime Minister, Prescott had been instrumental in negotiating the Kyoto Protocol, the groundbreaking international climate agreement signed in 1997, which sought to reduce global greenhouse gas emissions. The agreement was a landmark achievement for environmentalism, and Prescott's role in securing it cemented his reputation as a staunch advocate for climate action.

In the years following his retirement from active politics, Prescott continued to champion environmental causes, both in the UK and globally. He remained a vocal proponent of policies aimed at reducing carbon emissions, promoting renewable energy, and protecting natural resources.

He saw climate change as one of the most pressing issues facing humanity, and he believed that political leaders had a responsibility to take bold action to combat it. Prescott often spoke out about the dangers of climate denial and the need for greater global cooperation to address environmental challenges.

Beyond climate change, Prescott also remained deeply involved in social justice causes. He consistently spoke on issues such as poverty, inequality, and workers' rights, continuing the fight he had started during his political career. He understood that social change and environmental sustainability were interconnected, and he advocated for policies that addressed both. Prescott's post-political activism reflected his enduring belief in a fairer, more equitable world, and he remained a passionate voice for the marginalized throughout his retirement.

Prescott's advocacy also extended to the importance of international cooperation. He frequently expressed concern about the widening gap between rich and poor countries and the need for developed nations to support developing countries in the fight against climate change.

His work in global forums, his advocacy for renewable energy, and his involvement in charitable causes continued to underscore his deep commitment to making the world a better place. Even in retirement, Prescott remained a key figure in the fight for social and environmental justice, drawing on his extensive experience in government and his genuine desire to help the most vulnerable.

Reflections on the House of Lords and Retirement

In 2010, John Prescott was granted a life peerage and made a member of the House of Lords. This was a significant moment in his post-political career, offering him a new platform to contribute to public life. Although his role in the Lords was more ceremonial than his active participation as Deputy Prime Minister, Prescott took his position seriously. He believed that the House of Lords could still play an important role in scrutinizing legislation and ensuring that the voices of the people were heard in the corridors of power.

However, Prescott's time in the House of Lords was marked by his increasing health struggles. After suffering a stroke in 2019, his physical and mental well-being began to decline, and his ability to engage in parliamentary business became limited.

He spoke openly about the challenges he faced with his health and his subsequent decision to gradually withdraw from public life. Although he had not been an active participant in the House of Lords for some time, Prescott's legacy in the Lords remained one of advocacy for social justice, workers' rights, and climate change.

Despite his diminished capacity for parliamentary work, Prescott remained committed to the values that had defined his life. He continued to express his views through writing and public speeches, particularly on matters of social justice, the welfare state, and global issues. He reflected on his long political career and his role in shaping the modern Labour Party, and he was proud of the work he had done to improve the lives of working people, secure environmental protections, and fight for a fairer society.

Retirement did not mean a retreat for Prescott; it simply meant a shift in how he engaged with the world. He found new ways to contribute to society and continued to advocate for the causes he cared most about. Through public appearances, interviews, and his occasional participation in discussions, he remained a vocal presence in debates about the future of Britain and the world. For Prescott, retirement was not about stepping away from public life entirely but about finding new avenues to influence and inspire others.

Health Struggles: The Stroke and Alzheimer's Battle

As John Prescott entered his later years, his health began to deteriorate, marking the final chapter of his life in a difficult and poignant way. In 2019, he suffered a debilitating stroke, which affected his ability to perform daily tasks and curtailed his ability to actively participate in political or public life. The stroke left Prescott with physical challenges, including difficulty walking and speaking, and it became a turning point in his life, forcing him to confront the reality of aging and illness.

Despite his struggles, Prescott remained determined and resilient. Known for his tough persona and unwavering spirit throughout his career, he faced his health challenges with the same determination that had characterized his political life. Family, friends, and former colleagues reported that Prescott maintained his sharp sense of humor and his passion for social issues, even as his body weakened. His public appearances became increasingly rare, and he took a step back from public life, focusing on his health and spending time with his loved ones.

In addition to the stroke, Prescott's health further declined as he battled Alzheimer's disease. The onset of Alzheimer's, a cruel and progressive illness that affects memory and cognitive function, marked a tragic end to the vibrant political life of a man who had been known for his sharp intellect and dynamic personality.

John Prescott Biography

Prescott's family revealed that the former Deputy Prime Minister had struggled with the disease for some time before his passing in November 2024. His Alzheimer's diagnosis deeply affected his family, but they took comfort in the knowledge that Prescott had lived a life full of purpose, advocacy, and service to others.

Alzheimer's was a particularly cruel diagnosis for someone who had spent his life advocating for others, using his voice to influence policy and change. It also marked a difficult personal journey for Prescott's family, as they watched a man who had been so influential in politics gradually lose his memory and his ability to communicate. His family remained steadfast by his side, offering support and love as he fought the disease. Despite the toll it took on his body and mind, Prescott's loved ones expressed their deep pride in his legacy and the impact he had made in their lives and in the world.

Throughout these later years, Prescott's family and friends continued to celebrate the man he had been—his achievements, his commitment to social justice, his tough yet compassionate persona, and his lifelong dedication to public service. Though his health may have deteriorated, his legacy remained strong, and it was clear that the principles he had fought for during his political career would continue to inspire future generations.

Prescott's struggle with illness did not overshadow the tremendous impact he had on British politics and the lives of the people he championed, and his legacy lives on as a testament to his tireless advocacy for the common good.

In the final months of his life, Prescott was surrounded by his family, listening to his beloved jazz music, a fitting reminder of the man who had navigated the corridors of power with a unique combination of toughness and tenderness. His passing marked the end of an era in British politics, but his contributions—both in and out of government—continue to resonate today.

CHAPTER NINE

Tributes and Legacy

When John Prescott passed away in November 2024, his former colleagues, including two of the most significant figures in his political life—Tony Blair and Gordon Brown—were among the first to express their deep sorrow and pay tribute to his immense contributions to both the Labour Party and British politics.

Tony Blair, who served as Prime Minister from 1997 to 2007 and worked closely with Prescott for the entirety of his tenure, expressed profound sadness at the news of his passing. Blair referred to Prescott as "one of the most talented people I ever encountered in politics."

He recalled the working-class authenticity that Prescott brought to the heart of New Labour, offering a voice to a constituency that had felt increasingly disconnected from the establishment.

The bond between Blair and Prescott, despite their stark personal differences—Prescott was the tough, no-nonsense working-class figure, while Blair came from a more privileged, academic background—was built on mutual respect. Blair noted that Prescott's blunt style of communication and his unyielding dedication to his values made him a figure whose role in Labour's electoral success could never be overstated.

Blair also reminisced about their political collaboration, calling it "an odd couple" dynamic—Prescott, the "maverick" deputy who often acted as the party's anchor, and Blair, the more modernising force who led the party toward the political centre. Together, their partnership proved pivotal in winning three consecutive terms for Labour. Blair's tribute emphasized Prescott's ability to connect with voters who felt unheard, as well as his fierce loyalty to the party's working-class roots.

For Blair, John Prescott wasn't just a colleague but a friend whose memory he would cherish. He acknowledged Prescott's unwavering commitment to social justice and his integral role in the success of New Labour, stressing that the Labour Party would not have been as successful as it was without his contributions.

Gordon Brown, who succeeded Tony Blair as Prime Minister, also spoke movingly of Prescott's legacy. Brown, who had a more complex relationship with Prescott—especially given the latter's role as a mediator between Blair and Brown—nonetheless recognised Prescott's unique ability to bridge divides, particularly between Labour's leadership and its traditional base.

Brown described Prescott as "a legend of the Labour Party" who became a figure of great influence, not just within the party but across the broader political landscape. He praised Prescott for his loyalty to the Labour cause and his determination to represent working-class communities.

Brown also acknowledged Prescott's strong stance on social justice, which had always been one of his most defining features. Prescott's insistence on maintaining the Labour Party's commitment to social equity and fairness made him an enduring figure in British politics.

In reflecting on Prescott's death, Brown described him as someone who was able to connect with ordinary people in a way that few other politicians could. For Brown, Prescott's legacy would be one of enduring authenticity and a genuine commitment to representing the working class, ensuring their voices were heard in the halls of power.

He also spoke fondly of Prescott's larger-than-life personality, recalling his fiery speeches and his no-holds-barred approach to politics, which Brown said was a "breath of fresh air" during their time in office.

Both Blair and Brown's tributes underscored Prescott's extraordinary impact on both the Labour Party and British politics as a whole, highlighting how his legacy would live on through the policies he championed, the causes he fought for, and the people he inspired.

International Recognition: Al Gore's Testimony

While John Prescott was a deeply influential figure in British politics, his impact was also felt internationally, particularly in the realm of environmental policy. One of the most profound tributes came from Al Gore, the former Vice President of the United States and a long-time advocate for climate action. Al Gore and Prescott had worked closely together during the negotiation of the Kyoto Protocol in 1997, where Prescott played a critical role in securing the landmark international agreement to address climate change.

Gore, who had championed global environmental efforts, spoke of Prescott's dedication to environmental sustainability, his ability to unite diverse groups of stakeholders, and his unwavering commitment to addressing one of the world's most urgent challenges: climate change.

In his tribute, Gore said, "I have never worked with anyone in politics—on my side of the pond or his—quite like John Prescott." He described Prescott as a man who understood both the science of climate change and the practical realities of implementing policy. Gore recalled their many discussions on the international stage, where Prescott's insights and determination made him a crucial partner in the fight for environmental protections.

Gore appreciated Prescott's no-nonsense attitude and his ability to speak plainly, a trait that allowed him to cut through the bureaucracy and red tape that often hampered meaningful action. For Gore, Prescott was not just a colleague but a friend whose passion for the environment and social justice was contagious.

Gore further highlighted Prescott's unique ability to make the case for climate action to a broad audience, including working-class communities, many of whom felt the economic pressures of environmental policies. Prescott was able to forge connections with these groups, ensuring that climate policies did not alienate those who were most vulnerable to economic hardship. His advocacy for a just transition—one that would lift up working people while protecting the environment—was a core part of his environmental legacy.

In an era when global environmental challenges remain as pressing as ever, Gore noted that Prescott's work on climate change, especially through the Kyoto Protocol, was an enduring reminder of the power of international cooperation and the need for leaders to take bold, decisive action to protect the planet. Gore's tribute to Prescott served as a reminder that, while Prescott was a key figure in British politics, his legacy as an environmental advocate was also deeply felt across the world.

The Lasting Impact on Labour and British Politics

John Prescott's death left a void in the Labour Party, but his legacy continues to shape the party and British politics as a whole. Prescott's role in the rise of New

Labour, his defence of working-class values, and his determination to bridge the gap between the old and the new Labour movements ensured that his impact would be felt for generations.

Prescott was a man who firmly believed in the power of government to create positive change, particularly in improving the lives of working-class citizens, and his contributions to the political landscape of the UK continue to resonate today.

His influence can still be seen in the current political climate, where issues like social justice, inequality, and climate change remain central to the national discourse. The modern Labour Party, under the leadership of figures like Keir Starmer and

Angela Rayner, continues to reflect some of the core values that Prescott championed: a commitment to social equity, a focus on climate change, and an understanding of the needs of working-class communities.

Starmer and Rayner's leadership has often been compared to that of Prescott's era, with Starmer being seen as the political heir to Blair and Rayner taking on the role of a working-class voice within the party, much as Prescott had done decades earlier.

Moreover, Prescott's defence of Jeremy Corbyn's leadership during his tenure as Labour leader highlighted his lasting influence on the party. Despite their differences, Prescott understood the importance of unity within the party and the need to continue the fight for social justice, even when facing political divisions. His support for Corbyn demonstrated his belief in the necessity of maintaining the ideological integrity of the Labour Party, regardless of political trends.

Prescott's legacy is not confined to his role in the New Labour years, though. He will be remembered as a figure who brought authenticity to British politics—a working-class hero who never lost sight of the values that had shaped his life. From his early days as a merchant seaman and trade union activist to his time as Deputy Prime Minister and beyond, Prescott's unwavering commitment to his principles and to the people he served made him a giant in the political landscape.

In the years following his death, it is clear that Prescott's influence will continue to be felt. His legacy as a fighter for social justice, a champion for the environment, and a man who worked tirelessly to ensure that the voices of the working class were heard will remain a lasting inspiration for future generations of political leaders.

CHAPTER TEN

Lessons from a Life of Service

John Prescott's life story is a testament to the power of resilience and perseverance. From his humble beginnings in Prestatyn, Wales, to becoming one of the most prominent figures in British politics, Prescott's journey was not without its trials and challenges.

Yet, throughout his career, he demonstrated an extraordinary ability to face adversity head-on, remain steadfast in his beliefs, and continue his work in the face of personal and professional setbacks. His life offers valuable lessons on the importance of resilience in the pursuit of one's goals and ideals.

John Prescott Biography

One of the most significant challenges Prescott faced was his rise from a working-class background, where opportunities were limited, to the highest levels of government. As the son of a railwayman and the grandson of a miner, Prescott was acutely aware of the obstacles that working-class individuals faced in a society that often favored the elite.

But he never allowed these barriers to define him. He worked hard to build a career, first as a merchant seaman, then as a trade unionist, and finally as a Member of Parliament. Prescott's life illustrates the importance of perseverance in overcoming obstacles—whether it be societal limitations, personal struggles, or political opposition.

Prescott's resilience was also evident in his response to the many personal and professional setbacks he encountered. For example, in 2019, after suffering a stroke, Prescott's health began to decline significantly, and he had to step away from active politics. Despite his health challenges, he remained committed to public service, continuing to advocate for causes he cared deeply about, such as social justice and the environment.

Even as his physical and cognitive abilities deteriorated due to Alzheimer's disease in his later years, Prescott's family and close friends spoke of his determination to remain connected to the world around him, showing a resilience that defined both his public and private life.

Moreover, Prescott's ability to maintain his composure and determination despite public controversies, including the infamous egg incident in 2001, further exemplifies his resilience.

Though often criticized for his outspokenness and fiery temper, Prescott's steadfastness in fighting for the causes he believed in—whether it was the working class, environmental protection, or social justice—remains one of his most defining characteristics. His resilience under pressure, and his refusal to back down in the face of adversity, offers a powerful example of how one can stand firm for what is right, even when the odds are stacked against them.

In today's fast-paced and often divisive political climate, Prescott's example serves as a reminder that resilience is a key quality for any leader. His ability to weather the storms of both public and private life demonstrates that success is not defined by a lack of setbacks but by the ability to persevere in the face of them.

The Importance of Authenticity in Leadership

John Prescott's authenticity was one of his most enduring qualities. Throughout his political career, he remained unapologetically himself, never trying to fit into the mold of what others expected him to be. In a world of polished political speeches and carefully curated public personas, Prescott stood out for his honesty, bluntness, and, at times, his raw authenticity. His example shows how being true to oneself is not only valuable but essential in leadership.

Prescott's authenticity was evident in both his personal and political life. His background as a working-class man, with no pretense of intellectual or aristocratic privilege, made him an accessible figure to many. As a former merchant seaman and trade unionist, Prescott never lost touch with the experiences of ordinary people, and he wore his background as a badge of honor.

He did not try to hide his roots or pretend to be something he was not. His straightforward manner and lack of political finesse often drew criticism from those who viewed him as too blunt or unrefined. Yet, for many in the Labour Party and beyond, it was this very authenticity that made Prescott a relatable and trusted figure.

Prescott's authenticity was also displayed in his willingness to challenge his own party when he believed it was straying from its core values. His decision to speak out against the Iraq War, for instance, demonstrated his commitment to his principles, even when it meant disagreeing with his own colleagues. In a time when many politicians follow the party line without question, Prescott's independence of thought and willingness to act on his convictions made him stand out as a leader who truly believed in the causes he fought for.

John Prescott Biography

Another key moment that showcased Prescott's authenticity was his famous response to an egg thrown at him during a campaign visit in 2001. While his punch in retaliation became a highly publicized incident, it also symbolized his genuine frustration with those who sought to undermine him or his message.

Prescott's actions were a reflection of his passion and his commitment to standing up for himself and the values he represented, regardless of the opinions of others. In the world of politics, where image is often prioritized over substance, Prescott's willingness to show his true self, even in moments of controversy, remains a powerful lesson in the importance of authenticity.

For future leaders, Prescott's example teaches that authenticity is not a weakness but a strength. In an era of public scrutiny and media manipulation, being true to oneself and one's values can be the foundation of trust and long-term success. Prescott's genuine nature made him a beloved figure to many, and it allowed him to build real connections with the people he served. For leaders looking to make a lasting impact, following Prescott's example of authenticity could be the key to gaining the respect and admiration of those they seek to lead.

What Future Leaders Can Learn from John Prescott

John Prescott's life and career offer invaluable lessons for future leaders, not just in politics but in any field where leadership is key. From his resilience in the face of adversity to his commitment to social justice and environmental causes, Prescott's legacy provides a blueprint for leaders who want to make a meaningful difference.

One of the primary lessons that future leaders can learn from Prescott is the importance of staying true to one's roots. Prescott's working-class background was central to his political identity, and it was this identity that allowed him to connect with the people he represented. In a political landscape often dominated by elites and the privileged, Prescott's ability to stay grounded in his working-class origins made him a voice for the voiceless.

Future leaders should remember that leadership is not about distancing oneself from one's past but embracing it and using it as a source of strength. Leaders who connect with their communities on a personal level and understand the struggles of those they serve are far more likely to inspire loyalty and trust.

Another key takeaway from Prescott's life is the importance of courage in leadership. Prescott was never afraid to take a stand, even when it meant going against the grain or making unpopular decisions. Whether it was his opposition to the Iraq War, his staunch support for the working class, or his advocacy for environmental causes, Prescott demonstrated that true leadership requires the willingness to make tough choices, even when those choices come with significant political cost. For future leaders, this means having the courage to stand up for what is right, even in the face of opposition, and making decisions based on values rather than expediency.

Prescott also showed the value of being a mediator in times of conflict. His role in navigating the complex relationship between Tony Blair and Gordon Brown is an example of how a leader can bring opposing factions together to achieve common goals. In a world where politics is often defined by division and gridlock, future leaders can learn from Prescott's ability to negotiate and mediate, ensuring that different voices are heard and that progress is made even when tensions run high. Leadership is not just about being decisive; it's also about bringing people together and finding solutions that benefit the greater good.

Finally, Prescott's life reminds us that leadership requires empathy and humility. Despite his political prominence, Prescott never lost sight of the people he served. He remained deeply connected to his community, often returning to Hull and using his position to advocate for the issues that mattered most to his constituents.

For future leaders, this means not only making decisions that benefit the broader public but also ensuring that the voices of those most affected by those decisions are heard. Prescott's humility, despite his many achievements, demonstrated that effective leadership is rooted in a deep sense of service to others.

In conclusion, John Prescott's life provides a wealth of lessons for those who aspire to lead. From his resilience in the face of adversity to his authenticity, courage, and empathy, Prescott's example remains a powerful guide for anyone seeking to make a lasting impact. Future leaders can look to Prescott's career as a reminder that leadership is not just about power or position; it's about staying true to one's values, fighting for the greater good, and always striving to connect with the people one serves.

CONCLUSION

Summing Up a Life Well-Lived

John Prescott's life and legacy are a powerful testament to the impact one person can have on the world around them. As one of the longest-serving and most influential deputy prime ministers in British history, Prescott's journey was not only marked by his political achievements but by the depth of his commitment to social justice, environmental causes, and the working-class people he represented.

From his early days in Prestatyn, Wales, to his final years spent battling health issues, Prescott's unwavering dedication to public service paints a portrait of a man whose life was truly well-lived.

John Prescott Biography

His story is one of resilience, authenticity, and service, qualities that allowed him to overcome the odds and make an indelible mark on British politics. Prescott's rise from a working-class background to the highest echelons of power is nothing short of remarkable.

Despite the many challenges he faced—whether personal, professional, or political—he never wavered in his commitment to the causes he cared about. He devoted his life to improving the lives of others, fighting for social justice, and protecting the environment, leaving behind a legacy that will continue to inspire future generations of leaders.

Prescott's legacy is not just defined by his time in government or his role in shaping the New Labour movement but by his authenticity and his relentless advocacy for the values he held dear. Whether it was in his role as a mediator between Tony Blair and Gordon Brown or his advocacy for the Kyoto Protocol, Prescott always remained true to himself and his principles. His ability to connect with ordinary people, his passion for social causes, and his capacity for both compassion and blunt honesty made him a unique and unforgettable figure in British politics.

The Enduring Influence of John Prescott

Though John Prescott is no longer with us, his influence on British politics and society endures. His contributions to the Labour Party, his pivotal role in shaping policies on climate change, transport, and social justice, and his dedication to the working-class communities he represented will continue to be felt for years to come. Prescott's work in negotiating the Kyoto Protocol, his environmental advocacy, and his fight for social equality have left a lasting legacy in British political history, ensuring that his contributions are remembered long after his passing.

Prescott's influence extended beyond the United Kingdom, as evidenced by his work on international climate change treaties and his relationships with key global figures, such as former U.S. Vice President Al Gore.

His ability to connect with people from all walks of life, his straightforward approach to politics, and his dedication to making the world a better place made him a figure of global significance. Even as the political landscape evolved, Prescott's ability to stay grounded in his working-class roots and maintain a focus on social justice ensured that his voice remained a powerful one, resonating with people from all backgrounds.

In the modern political world, where the divide between the political elite and ordinary citizens often seems insurmountable, Prescott's legacy is a reminder of the importance of authenticity and connection. His career was a shining example of how politics can be used as a force for good, particularly when driven by a genuine desire to improve the lives of others. Future leaders can look to Prescott's life as a model of how to navigate the complexities of modern politics while staying true to one's values and connecting with the people one serves.

Prescott's long tenure in the House of Commons and his significant influence on key national and international issues have solidified his place in history. But it's not just his political achievements that will be remembered. It's the way he carried himself, the way he was able to speak for those who often went unheard, and the way he represented the underdog that makes his legacy enduring. Prescott's influence is not just something that will be found in the history books—it's something that continues to shape the future of the Labour Party and British politics as a whole.

Carrying Forward His Fight for Justice and Equality

While John Prescott may no longer be in active politics, his fight for justice, equality, and social change lives on through the work of those who continue to carry his torch. Prescott was a tireless advocate for the working class, for the marginalized, and for the environment.

His dedication to social justice, his unflinching support for the underprivileged, and his role in driving significant policy reforms all stand as a reminder of the kind of world he strived to build. In a time when political figures often prioritize the interests of the elite, Prescott's unwavering commitment to the needs of ordinary people offers a guiding light for anyone who seeks to create a more just and equitable society.

One of the most enduring aspects of Prescott's legacy is his belief in the power of community. He never lost sight of the people he represented—whether it was the constituents of Hull or the working-class communities across the country. His life was a testament to the idea that politics should serve the people, and that leaders should never forget their roots. This is a lesson that remains as relevant today as it was during his time in office. In an era of increasing political division and growing inequality, Prescott's example reminds us of the importance of unity, compassion, and solidarity in shaping a better future.

Prescott's work on environmental issues, particularly his involvement in the Kyoto Protocol, also continues to resonate in the context of today's global climate crisis. His efforts to push for meaningful action on climate change laid the groundwork for future environmental policies and have inspired a new generation of leaders who are committed to protecting the planet. As the world grapples with the effects of climate change, Prescott's advocacy for global cooperation and environmental responsibility remains a touchstone for anyone working to address this critical issue.

Similarly, Prescott's commitment to social justice and his belief in the power of the Labour Party to bring about positive change continue to shape the political discourse in the United Kingdom. His steadfast support for policies that promote equality, fairness, and opportunity has left an indelible mark on the Labour movement. Though the political landscape may have changed, the values that Prescott championed—social justice, workers' rights, and environmental stewardship—remain central to the party's mission and vision for the future.

In this sense, Prescott's legacy is far from over. His life serves as a call to action for all who care about justice and equality, urging us to continue the fight for a better world. Whether it's through political action, social advocacy, or environmental efforts, Prescott's spirit lives on in the work of those who follow in his footsteps.

His example reminds us that true leadership is about more than achieving personal success—it's about making a meaningful difference in the lives of others and leaving a positive legacy for future generations.

In conclusion, John Prescott's life was one of profound service, lasting impact, and unwavering commitment to the principles of justice and equality. As we reflect on his achievements and his enduring influence, we are reminded of the power of authenticity, resilience, and a deep commitment to the greater good.

John Prescott Biography

Prescott's legacy will continue to inspire those who strive to build a fairer, more just society, and his fight for justice and equality will carry on through the actions of future generations of leaders.

THANKS FOR READING!!!

www.ingramcontent.com/pod-product-compliance
Ingram Content Group UK Ltd.
Pitfield, Milton Keynes, MK11 3LW, UK
UKHW032213171224
452513UK00010B/575